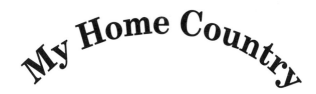

VIETNAM

IS MY HOME

For a free color catalog describing Gareth Stevens' list of high-quality books, call 1-800-341-3569 (USA) or 1-800-461-9120 (Canada).

For their help in the preparation of *My Home Country: Vietnam is My Home*, the writer and editor gratefully thank Boi Ngoc Nguyen and all the children of Vietnam.

Flag illustration on page 42, © Flag Research Center.

Library of Congress Cataloging-in-Publication Data

Wright, David K.
    Vietnam is my home / adapted from Patricia Norland's Children of the world—Vietnam by David Wright ; photographs by Vu Viet Dung.
       p. cm. — (My home country)
    Includes bibliographical references and index.
    Summary: Presents the life of an eleven-year-old girl and her family in Vietnam, describing her home and school activities and discussing the history, geography, ethnic composition, languages, culture, and other aspects of her country.
    ISBN 0-8368-0905-X
    1. Vietnam—Juvenile literature. 2. Children—Vietnam—Juvenile literature. [1. Vietnam. 2. Family life—Vietnam.]
I. Vu, Viet Dung, ill. II. Norland, Patricia. Vietnam. III. Title. IV. Series.
DS556.3.W76 1993
959.7—dc20
                92-34674

Edited, designed, and produced by

Gareth Stevens Publishing
1555 North RiverCenter Drive, Suite 201
Milwaukee, Wisconsin 53212, USA

Text, photographs, and format copyright 1993 by Gareth Stevens, Inc. First published in the United States and Canada in 1993 by Gareth Stevens, Inc. This US edition is abridged from *Children of the World: Vietnam*, copyright 1991 by Gareth Stevens, Inc., with text by Patricia Norland and photographs by Vu Viet Dung.

Series editors: Barbara J. Behm and Beth Karpfinger
Research editor: Kathleen Weisfeld Barrilleaux
Cover design: Kristi Ludwig
Layout: Kate Kriege
Map design: Sheri Gibbs

Printed in the United States of America

1 2 3 4 5 6 7 8 9 96 95 94 93

My Home Country

VIETNAM

IS MY HOME

Adapted from Patricia Norland's
Children of the World: Vietnam
by David Wright
Photographs by Vu Viet Dung

Gareth Stevens Publishing
MILWAUKEE

Ho thi Kim Chau is an 11-year-old girl who lives with her family in a tiny village outside of Ho Chi Minh City in Vietnam. She takes care of the family animals and enjoys playing games with her friends. Chau also likes to visit the big city located ten miles away.

To enhance this book's value in libraries and classrooms, clear and simple reference sections include up-to-date information about Vietnam's history, land and climate, people and language, education, and religion. *Vietnam Is My Home* also features a large and colorful map, bibliography, glossary, simple index, research topics, and activity projects designed especially for young readers.

The living conditions and experiences of children in Vietnam vary according to economic, environmental, and ethnic circumstances. The reference sections help bring to life for young readers the diversity and richness of the culture and heritage of Vietnam. Of particular interest are discussions of Vietnam's government, natural resources, cultural life, and its long and interesting history.

My Home Country includes the following titles:

Canada	*Nicaragua*
Costa Rica	*Peru*
Cuba	*Poland*
El Salvador	*South Africa*
Guatemala	*Vietnam*
Ireland	*Zambia*

CONTENTS

LIVING IN VIETNAM:
Chau, a Country Girl

Ho thi Kim Chau is 11 years old. She lives with her family in a tiny village in Vietnam, near the country's biggest city. The city used to be called Saigon but is now called Ho Chi Minh City.

There are many things for Chau to do each day. She can play with family pets, play games, see friends, or visit relatives. Her village has green fields of rice and pretty gardens between the houses.

Ho thi Kim Chau is 11 years old. Like most Vietnamese, she lives in the country. Her home is in a tiny village. ▶

North America

South America

Europe

Asia

Africa

Vietnam

Australia

Socialist Republic of Vietnam

China

Myanmar (Burma)

Hanoi

Laos

Thailand

Cambodia

Ho Chi Minh City

South China Sea

Vietnam is a rice-growing nation. Planting rice is hard work.

Chau and Her Family

Chau's father's name is Nho. Three nights a week, he works as a security guard at a paper factory. At home, his duties include working in the family garden and feeding the family's many chickens and ducks.

Muoi is Chau's mother. She is a home-maker. Nho's parents work as gardeners. Muoi's parents are carpenters.

This is Chau's family. The entire family gets together often at her house for meals.

Vietnamese travel rivers and streams in boats called *sampans*.

Chau helps her mother with the dishes.

◀ Muoi needs help from her daughters to do all the chores.

In Vietnam, last names are first, and first names are last! In Ho thi Kim Chau's name, *Ho* is the family name of her father. *Chau* is her first name. Names also have meaning. *Chau* means "gemstone" in Vietnamese. *Muoi* means "ten" in Vietnamese.

When Chau grows up, she wants to be like Muoi, her mother.

At Home

Chau's parents built their house in 1983. A big river runs behind the house. Sugarcane grows in nearby fields. A dozen palm trees stand in front of the house. Coconut and eucalyptus trees shade Chau's path to the main road.

The house has two rooms. The larger room is used as the living area, bedroom, and sewing area. The smaller room is used as the kitchen and dining area.

Chau's home is larger than homes in Vietnam's big cities. ▶
Chau and her sister, Loan, play in a hammock.

Chau helps her sisters do their homework.

When she is not wearing her *ao dai*, Chau's grandmother likes to wear loose-fitting, pajama-type clothing. ▶

Chau spends most mornings doing her schoolwork. In her spare time, she likes to sew. Someday, she wants to sew as well as her mother. Maybe then she will be able to make an *ao dai*. An ao dai is an outfit worn by Vietnamese women. It has two pieces — a long dress that is worn over a loose pair of long pants.

16

Daily Chores

Chau gets up at 6:00 each morning. After washing and dressing, she chops wood for a fire. At every meal, the family eats rice. Breakfast is boiled rice with meat or fish.

Vietnamese eat with large spoons or chopsticks.

Nho hauls water in pails from the river.

Right: Chau sweeps the kitchen. Metal pans and woven baskets hang on the wall.

After breakfast, Chau feeds the chickens and ducks. Water used by the family comes from the big river behind the house. Chau's father carries water in two big pails. River water is stored in a huge barrel beside the house. The water must be boiled before it is safe to drink. But water for bathing or for the garden can be taken from the barrels.

Some families live on fishing boats like these. Fishing is an important industry in Vietnam.

Chau does her homework each morning after chores. Later, she helps fix lunch. Twice a week, Chau takes care of her two sisters so her mother can go to the market. The three girls sometimes do the laundry by washing the clothes in buckets outside.

At the market, Muoi buys fruit called *vu sua*, or milk apple. She also buys *buoi* or *pomelo*, a grapefruit, plus *chom chom*, or *rambutan*, a sweet and juicy fruit.

Market vendors keep fruits and vegetables under umbrellas, out of the hot sun.

Chau's Pets

Chau and her family have many pets. One dog is named *Va,* which means "spotted." The other dog is named *Muc*, which means "black."

Chau's two best girlfriends are Nga and My. They talk, jump rope, and play house together. Chau and her family go to bed when it gets dark. They have no electricity.

One of Chau's favorite chores is feeding the ducks.

Playing with friends makes Chau happy.

Va sits quietly as Chau and her sisters play.

Chau's School Day

Chau eats an early lunch, then walks to school. She leaves her home at 11:30 a.m. School is one mile away. During the six-month rainy season, roads are muddy.

Most children go to free public schools. Almost all Vietnamese people learn to read and write.

Students wear school uniforms. Chau must wear a white shirt with a blue skirt or pants.

◄   Chau passes rice paddies on her way to school. The rice smells sweet and is ready to harvest.

Chau adds a hat to her school uniform because it shades her from the sun.

Chau's school is larger and newer than most schools in Vietnam.

At Chau's school, classes are very crowded, so children go to school in two shifts. One shift is from 7:30 to 11:30 a.m., and the other is from 1:00 to 4:30 p.m.

School is in session five days a week. There are no classes on Thursday or Sunday. Summer vacation is from June to August. Chau spends her vacation caring for her animals, helping her mother, and playing games with friends.

Teachers are well respected in Vietnam.

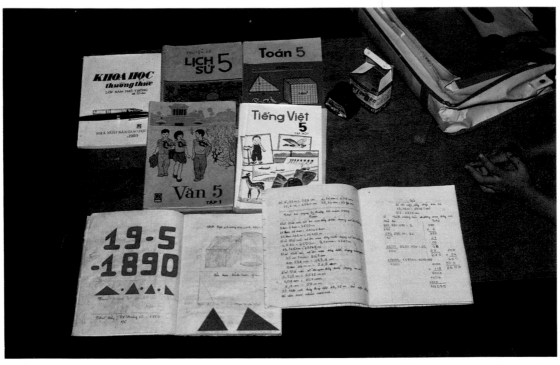

Shown are Chau's books for literature, science, history, and math.

Chau and her school friends laugh during the afternoon break.

Chau studies many subjects at school. She learns mathematics, reading, history, drawing, Vietnamese stories, science, manual work, and morals. Chau's favorite subject is reading.

Next year, in sixth grade, Chau will learn a foreign language. She can choose English, French, or Russian. In the Vietnamese language, words that are spelled the same can be said as many as six different ways.

Chau can be seen the fourth from the left in the front row.

Playing Games

Recess lasts 30 minutes. Students do exercises for the first 10 minutes. The other 20 minutes are for play. Chau and her friends like to jump rope, while the boys spin tops or play hide-and-seek. Vietnamese children also like to play jacks. Metal jacks and rubber balls are expensive, so the children use a lime and pieces of chopsticks.

The girls take on the boys in a tug of war. Instead of using a rope, team members grab the waist of the person in front of them.

Above: The first 10 minutes of recess are for exercises.

Right: These schoolboys gather water. Few buildings have running water.

Vendors sell pretty flowers in Ho Chi Minh City.

Visiting Ho Chi Minh City

The Ho family likes to visit Ho Chi Minh City. It has pretty streets and crowds of people. Chau likes seeing both the old and modern buildings.

Traffic is heavy in Ho Chi Minh City, and there seems to be a million bicycles! Three-wheeled bikes called *cyclos* serve as taxis for the city.

Three-wheeled cyclos are pedaled by a driver. Cyclos are the taxis of Vietnam.

Back home, Chau eats some of her favorite foods. She likes corn on the cob and sticky rice cooked in coconut milk. Her favorite drink is lemonade, and she also likes oranges. When Chau is sick, her mother gives her boiled-rice soup.

Meat and fish are often served with fish sauce. The sauce is called *nuoc mam*. It is made from a liquid created by putting salt and tiny fish in a barrel. The liquid drips into a bowl and is then mixed with garlic, lemon juice, sugar, or hot peppers.

Fresh fish is sold each day at the market.

Vietnamese dishes feature many fresh fruits and vegetables.

Customs and Festivals

The Vietnamese have many different religious customs. In Chau's home, there is an altar in one room. There, the Hos pay respect to close family members who have gone before them.

Most Vietnamese do not celebrate birthdays. But on her first birthday, Chau's family held a ceremony to show that she was old enough to leave the cradle.

Chau's father holds a burning stick of incense as the family members pray to their ancestors at the altar.

Ancestor worship takes place throughout Vietnam. Food is set out to share with relatives who have died.

Right: A photo of an ancestor hangs above this family altar.

Firecrackers tied to a tree explode during the Tet holiday.

Tet

Tet is Vietnam's most important holiday. It celebrates the start of the new year and the birth of spring.

During Tet, the Ho family visits a temple in Ho Chi Minh City to pray for a happy new year. Many people set off firecrackers to scare away evil spirits left from the old year.

Chau and her family go to plays and concerts during the celebration. This time helps Chau learn about her native culture.

During Tet, many people light firecrackers in celebration of the new year.

This celebration of Tet took place in a village in northern Vietnam.

MORE FACTS ABOUT: Vietnam

Official Name: Cong Hoa Xa Hoi Chu Nghia Viet Nam (kong wah zah hoy chu nwee VEE-et nahm), Socialist Republic of Vietnam

Capital: Hanoi

History

The first Vietnamese probably came from China 5,000 years ago. Many became fishers, hunters, or farmers.

By the end of the 19th century, France controlled Vietnam. After World War II, the Vietnamese fought against the French and, in 1954, forced them out. The leader of the revolt was Ho Chi Minh. The revolt split Vietnam into two countries — North Vietnam and South Vietnam. Ho and his followers in the north were communists. The South Vietnamese wanted democracy. When northerners came south to fight in 1960, the United States and others stepped in to help the south. American soldiers began to die in great numbers alongside the Vietnamese. By 1973, the US had pulled out of Vietnam. The war lasted for two more years, until the communist north claimed victory.

Today, the country of Vietnam is a communist country. The government controls the economy and runs all the industries.

Land and Climate

Vietnam is shaped like the letter *s*. Each end contains fertile river valleys with mountainous jungle in between. In the north, winters are rainy and cool. In the south, winters are dry and warm. Summers are hot and dry in the north and hot and wet in the south.

People and Language

There are about 70 million Vietnamese. Besides the native Vietnamese, there are Chinese, Khmer, and Thai. The people speak Vietnamese, French, or a Chinese language.

Education

School is free for the first 12 years. The country has three universities and more than 40 colleges and technical schools.

Religion

Not all Vietnamese are religious, but most people pay respect to their ancestors. Buddhism is the most common religion. Many have faith in what is known as geomancy. This is an ancient belief that everything should line up in its proper place or direction. Other religious influences include Taoism and Confucianism.

Vietnamese money before North and South Vietnam were reunified.

Sports and Recreation

Racket games such as tennis and badminton are popular, as is bicycling and swimming. Swimming can be done all year at the beaches located in southern and central Vietnam.

Vietnamese in North America

Since the end of the war in 1975, more than 165,000 Vietnamese have become United States citizens. North American cities with large Vietnamese communities include Los Angeles, Houston, San Diego, Vancouver, and Toronto.

Glossary of Useful Vietnamese Terms

chao (chow): hello and good-bye

con gai (KAWN guy): girl

con trai (KAWN try): boy

lua (LOO-ah): rice

truong (TROO-uhn): school

More Books about Vietnam

Vietnam. Coley (Chelsea House)
Vietnam. Wright (Childrens Press)

Things to Do

1. On one list, tell how your life is like Chau's. On another, tell how it is different. Which list is longer?

2. If you would like a Vietnamese pen pal, write to Worldwide Pen Friends, P.O. Box 39097, Downey, CA 90241.

Be sure to tell them what country you want your pen pal to be from. Also include your full name, age, and address.

VIETNAM – Political and Physical

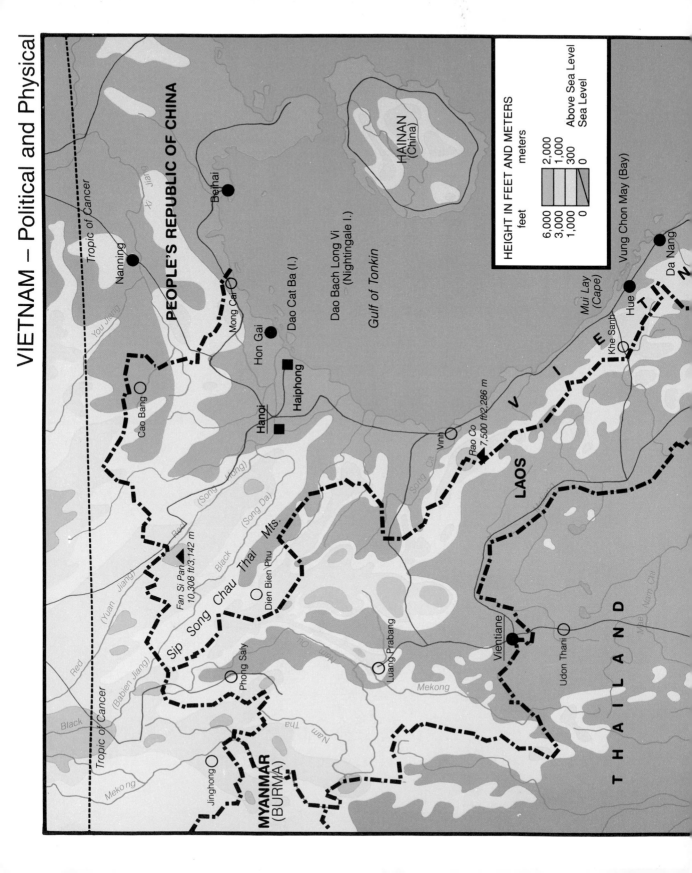

PEOPLE'S REPUBLIC OF CHINA

HAINAN
(China)

Gulf of Tonkin

Dao Bach Long Vi
(Nightingale I.)

Dao Cat Ba (I.)

Belhai

Nanning

Tropic of Cancer

Mong Cai

Hon Gai

Haiphong

Hanoi

Cao Bang

You Jiang

Xi Jiang

(Song Hong)

(Song Da)

Red

Black

(Yuan Jiang)

(Babien Jiang)

Fan Si Pan
10,308 ft/3,142 m

Sip Song Chau Thai Mts.

Dien Bien Phu

Phong Saly

Jinghong

Mekong

Red

Black

MYANMAR
(BURMA)

Nam Tha

Nam Ou

Luang Prabang

Mekong

Vientiane

Udon Thani

T H A I L A N D

Mae Nam Chi

LAOS

Vinh

Rao Co
7,500 ft/2,286 m

Song Ca

V I E T N A M

Khe Sanh

Mui Lay
(Cape)

Hue

Vung Chon May (Bay)

Da Nang

Tropic of Cancer

HEIGHT IN FEET AND METERS
feet   meters

6,000   2,000   Above Sea Level
3,000   1,000
1,000   300   Sea Level
0   0

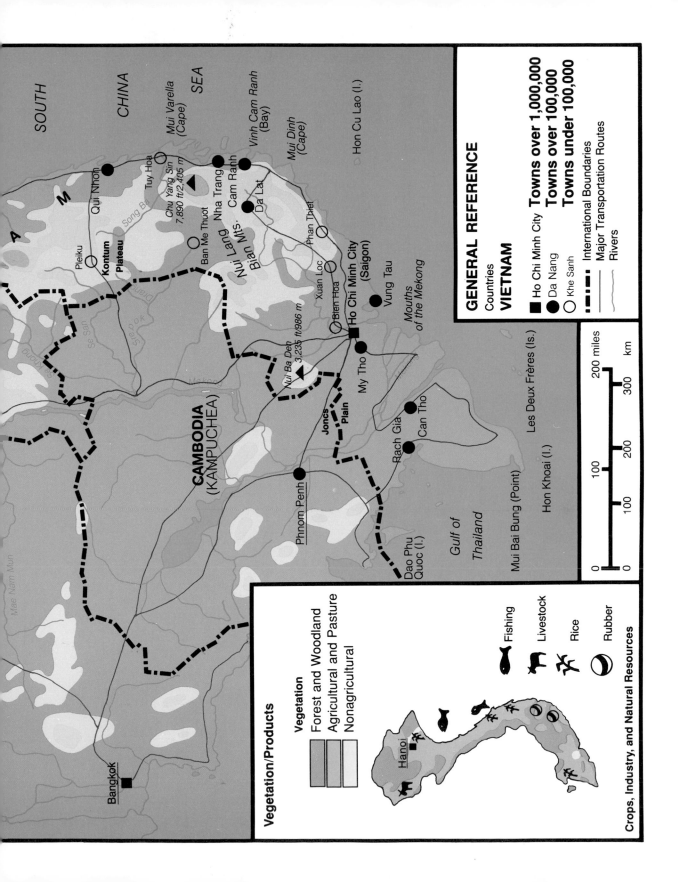

GENERAL REFERENCE

Countries
VIETNAM

■ Ho Chi Minh City **Towns over 1,000,000**

● Da Nang **Towns over 100,000**

○ Khe Sanh **Towns under 100,000**

▬▪▬▪ International Boundaries

Major Transportation Routes

Rivers

200 miles

100   100   200

0   100   200   300   km

Vegetation/Products

Vegetation

Forest and Woodland

Agricultural and Pasture

Nonagricultural

🐟 Fishing

🐂 Livestock

🌾 Rice

◐ Rubber

Crops, Industry, and Natural Resources

SOUTH

CHINA

SEA

Mui Varella (Cape)

Vinh Cam Ranh (Bay)

Mui Dinh (Cape)

Hon Cu Lao (I.)

Qui Nhon

Tuy Hoa

Chu Yang Sin 7,890 ft/2,405 m ▲

Nha Trang

Cam Ranh

Da Lat

Phan Thiet

Ban Me Thuot

Nui Lang Bian Mts.

Pleiku

Kontum Plateau

Song Ba

Se San

Srepok

Mekong

Xuan Loc

Bien Hoa

Nui Ba Den 3,235 ft/986 m ▲

Ho Chi Minh City (Saigon)

Vung Tau

Mouths of the Mekong

Les Deux Freres (Is.)

Joncs Plain

My Tho

Can Tho

Rach Gia

CAMBODIA (KAMPUCHEA)

Phnom Penh

Dao Phu Quoc (I.)

Gulf of Thailand

Mui Bai Bung (Point)

Hon Khoai (I.)

Mae Nam Mun

Bangkok

Hanoi

Index